# Alien Jokes

## Sandy Ransford

Illustrated by **Jane Eccles**

MACMILLAN CHILDREN'S BOOKS

First published 2000
by Macmillan Children's Books
a division of Macmillan Publishers Ltd
25 Eccleston Place, London SW1W 9NF
Basingstoke and Oxford
www.macmillan.com

Associated companies throughout the world

ISBN 0 330 39219 0

3 5 7 9 8 6 4 2

A CIP catalogue record for this book is available from the British Library.

Printed by Mackays of Chatham plc, Chatham, Kent.

# Contents

Little Green Men 7

A Space Odyssey 15

Saucers Flying 25

Monstrous! 37

Star-studded 47

Other Worlds 55

Earthlings Strike Back 67

Aliens All 81

# Little Green Men

On which side is an alien green?
**The outside.**

What's green, toothless and wrinkled?
**An alien's grandad.**

FIRST ALIEN: You've got a face like a million dollars.
**SECOND ALIEN: Really?**
FIRST ALIEN: Yes, all green and wrinkled.

What's green and smells?
**An alien's nose.**

What's green and prickly?
**An alien who's
forgotten to shave.**

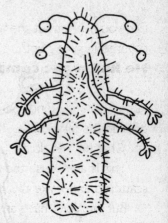

Why was the alien such a
good gardener?
**Because he had
green fingers.**

Where do Venusians get their milk?
**From milk craters.**

LITTLE ALIEN: When's dinner going to be ready?
**HIS MUM: You'll have to wait a while,
I've only got three pairs of hands.**

What's the difference between an alien and a banana?
**Try picking it up. If you can't, it's either an alien or a very large banana.**

How do you make an alien shrink?
**Feed it on condensed milk.**

How can you stop aliens from charging?
**Take away their credit cards.**

Did you hear about the alien who wanted to be covered in gold paint?
**He had a gilt complex.**

A man was scattering powder all over the pavement outside the post office. The shopkeeper came out to ask what he was doing.

'This is alien dust,' the man explained. 'If it's scattered about like this it will keep them away.'

'But we don't have any aliens round here,' said the astonished shopkeeper.

'There you are!' exclaimed the man. 'That just shows how well it works!'

What did the metric alien say?
**'Take me to your litre.'**

A lonely alien who had lived on Earth for a year after landing here by accident decided to advertise in the local paper for a girlfriend. He described himself as two metres tall, with two large green heads and three hands, each with ten fingers. But, he added, I'm kind and gentle and have a good sense of humour.

A lady responded to his advertisement. She said she thought personality was much more important than looks, and that she'd like to meet him on Thursday at 7 p.m. outside the town hall. 'Could you wear a red carnation in your buttonhole,' she added, 'just so I'll recognise you?'

What do you call a 3-metre-tall alien with four ears, each of which has a football sock stuffed in it?
**Anything you like, because he can't hear you!**

What do you call an overweight E.T.?
**An extra-cholesterol.**

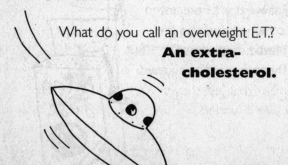

What should you do if you find a green alien?
**Wait until it ripens.**

What should you do if you find a blue alien?
**Try to cheer it up.**

What has two heads, four hands, four feet and a battery?
**An alien with spare parts.**

What would you do if you found yourself surrounded by a group of very scary alien space monsters?
**Hope you were at a fancy dress party.**

Two aliens landed on Earth right in the middle of a busy city street, and the first thing they spotted was a traffic light. One went over to talk to it.

'I saw her first,' protested the other.

'Maybe,' replied the first. 'But I'm the one she winked at.'

How does an alien make yogurt?
**He buys a pint of milk and stares at it.**

What do you call a friendly and good-looking alien?
**A failure.**

Where do Martians go for a drink?
**Mars bars.**

What should you do if an alien knocks on your front door?
**Run out of the back door!**

ALIEN, CONFRONTING EARTHLING: Don't be frightened, I don't have an enemy in the world.
**TERRIFIED EARTHLING: No, they're all in another world.**

An old lady stopped an alien in the street. 'You look like a nice young man,' she said. 'Can you tell me the way to the optician's?'

An alien wandering round the streets of London stopped a passer-by. 'Can you tell me if I'm right for the zoo?' he asked.

The passer-by looked at him. 'With your face, certainly,' he replied.

What do you get if you cross an alien with a group of athletes?
**A space race.**

TWENTY-THIRD CENTURY TEACHER: In 2250 aliens conquered Britain, France and Spain. Why did they stop there?
**PUPIL: Did they run out of conkers?**

What's an alien after it's twenty-one years old?
**Twenty-two years old.**

What do you get if you cross an alien with a wizard?
**A flying sorcerer.**

What happened to the alien who fell in a barrel of beer?
**He came to a bitter end.**

What do you get if you cross a little green man with a pig?
**A little green boar.**

An alien went into an Italian restaurant and ordered a pizza. He waited and waited, but still there was no sign of the food. Eventually he hailed a waiter.
'Excuse me,' he called out, 'but will my pizza be long?'
    'No, sir, round,' was the reply.

ALIEN: Aliens are smarter than Earthlings, you know.
**EARTHLING: I never knew that.**
ALIEN: See what I mean?

Knock, knock.
**Who's there?**
Cereal.
**Cereal who?**
Cereal pleasure to disintegrate you.

# A Space Odyssey

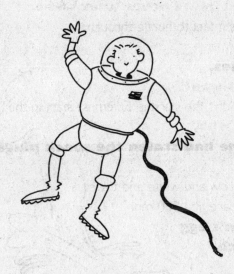

How many aliens can you cram into an empty space rocket?
**Only one. After that it isn't empty any more.**

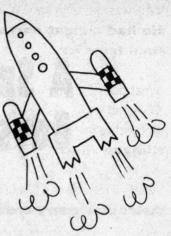

How can an alien avoid spaceship accidents?
**Stay at home.**

How does it feel to hurtle through space?
**It hurtles.**

Why wouldn't the starship *Enterprise* start in the morning?
**Someone had stolen the spock plugs.**

What's yellow and white and travels through space at 1,000 mph?
**An alien's egg sandwich.**

Why was the alien known as Captain Kirk?
**He had a right ear, a left ear and a final frontier.**

What does Captain Kirk wrap his sandwiches in?
**Klingon film.**

What's a spaceman's favourite game?
**Astronauts and crosses.**

What do you get if you cross a chip with a spaceship?
**An unidentified frying object.**

What holds the moon up in the sky?
**Moonbeams.**

Two aliens went into a bar on the moon for a drink but they left after about half an hour. They said it had no atmosphere.

Knock, knock.
**Who's there?**
Goose.
**Goose who?**
Goose who's just landed from outer space?

Knock, knock.
**Who's there?**
Bet.
**Bet who?**
Bet you never thought you'd
meet an alien!

Knock, knock.
**Who's there?**
Ma.
**Ma who?**
Ma-rtians aren't all little green men.

FIRST ALIEN: How old are you?
**SECOND ALIEN: 842, but I don't look
it, do I?**
FIRST ALIEN: No, but you used to.

SPACE TRAVELLER: Do you believe in free speech?
**ALIEN: Of course.**
SPACE TRAVELLER: Good, I need to borrow your
phone to make a call to Earth.

Why did the egg go to Mars?
**It was an egg-splorer.**

What do you call the planet Mr Spock didn't come from?
**Vulcan't.**

Do spaceships crash often?
**No, only once.**

What do you get if you cross a ram with a spaceship?
**The star sheep *Enterprise*.**

What did the group of stars win in the space race?
**A constellation prize.**

Knock, knock.
**Who's there?**
Rock.
**Rock who?**
Rock-et'll speed you to Planet Zygon.

How do you get a baby spaceship to go to sleep?
**Rocket.**

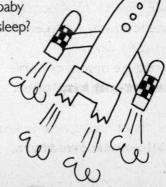

Knock, knock.
**Who's there?**
Cy.
**Cy who?**
Cybermen are knocking on your door.

A spaceman from Earth landed on Planet Zedon.
He asked the first alien he met, 'Can you tell me
how to get to the Xon space station from here?'
    The alien pondered for a few moments. 'Go
along this track for a few kilometres, then turn left at
the lake. Or is it right? No, it's left. Then go about
half a kilometre and take the
first left, no, the second left.
Then take the first right, no,
hang on, left again. Come to
think of it, if I were you and
wanted to get to the Xon
space station, I wouldn't
start from here at all.'

What should you
always carry when
exploring the deserts of Mars?
**A thirst-aid kit.**

What do astronauts wear to keep warm?
**Apollo-neck sweaters.**

Knock, knock.
**Who's there?**
Justin.
**Justin who?**
Justin time to catch the last spaceship home.

Why didn't the coward want to go into space?
**He suffered from atmos-fear.**

How do they forecast the weather on Mars?
**They hang a piece of string out of the window. When it moves, they know it's windy; when it's wet, they know it's raining.**

LONNIE: Do you know there's a star called the Dog Star?
**DONNIE: You can't be Sirius.**

Why did the young man become an astronaut?
**Because he was no Earthly good.**

A space traveller was having problems sorting out an insurance claim so he hired a lawyer. 'I'll give you £1,000 and you can do all my worrying over this case for me.'

'OK,' said the lawyer, 'where's the £1,000?'

'Ah,' replied the space traveller. 'That's your first worry.'

What did the space monster say when it saw two astronauts in a space buggy?
**'Ah, meals on wheels.'**

Which part of a space buggy is the laziest?
**The wheels, they're always tyred.**

SPACE INSTRUCTOR: You've got your space boots on the wrong feet.
**SPACE CADET: But they're the only feet I've got.**

Why was Johnny called the space cadet?
**Because he had a lot of space between his ears.**

Two astronauts landed on a faraway planet and spotted strange, and very large, footprints in the dust. 'Looks like some kind of giant beast,' said the first. 'I suppose we should try and track it down and see what it is.'

'Mmm,' replied his companion. 'I tell you what: you follow them to see where they go and I'll go back to see where they came from.'

SPACE TRAVELLER: I'd like to hire a space buggy, please.

**MARTIAN ATTENDANT: Certainly, sir, how long?**

SPACE TRAVELLER: The longest you've got, I've brought all my friends.

A space buggy driver asked his companion to get out so he could see if the indicators were working. 'Yes, no, yes, no, yes, no,' replied the friend.

During a rocket flight for tourists a voice came over the intercom: 'Ladies and gentlemen, we hope you enjoy your flight. Sit back and relax, everything on this ship is entirely automatic – the flight, the landing, even the restaurant service. Nothing can go wrong, nothing can go wrong, nothing can go wrong, nothing can go ...'

# Saucers
# Flying

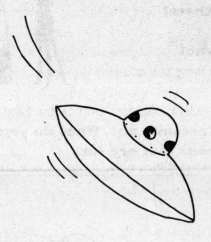

Two aliens landed their flying saucer in Britain and spotted a red pillar box. 'Take us to your leader,' said the first alien.

'Don't be daft,' said the second, 'it's no use talking to him, can't you see he's just a child?'

Knock, knock.
**Who's there?**
Olive.
**Olive who?**
Olive in a flying saucer.

YOUNG ALIEN: Dad, can I borrow the flying saucer?
**DAD: Certainly not. What do you think your feet are for?**
YOUNG ALIEN: One for the accelerator and one for the brake.

NEWSFLASH: Two flying saucers, one carrying red paint and one carrying blue paint, have crashed on Planet Zygon. The pilots are now marooned.

How do aliens drink tea?
**From flying saucers.**

Where do aliens leave their flying saucers?
**At parking meteors.**

NEWSFLASH: Two aliens are reported to have disembarked from a flying saucer which landed this afternoon in Surrey. Both are dressed in silver spacesuits; one is around three metres tall, the other only about one metre tall. Police are searching high and low for them.

FIRST ALIEN: I've been piloting this flying saucer for ten years and I've never had an accident.
**SECOND ALIEN: I suppose that makes you a wreckless pilot.**

Knock, knock.
**Who's there?**
Norma.
**Norma who?**
Norma Lee I travel by flying saucer but today I fancy a ride on a bus.

Knock, knock.
**Who's there?**
Warren.
**Warren who?**
Warren my spacesuit today.

When's an astronaut's main meal?
**Launch time.**

Knock, knock.
**Who's there?**
Arthur.
**Arthur who?**
Arthur any more aliens in that flying saucer?

What do you get if you cross an alien's spaceship with a chip pan?
**A frying saucer.**

What does UFO stand for in the school dining-room?
**Unidentified Frying Objects.**

Why did the jars of chopped mint and vinegar go up in a rocket?
**They wanted to be flying sauces.**

GILLY: Why do rockets fly so fast?
**BILLY: You'd fly fast if your tail was on fire.**

How can you spell an alien's enemies in four letters?
**FOES.**

A traveller from Mars walked into a bar in London and asked, 'Do you serve aliens?'

'Yes,' said the barman.

'Good,' replied the Martian. 'I'll have a glass of beer and an alien sandwich, please.'

Some aliens who landed in the Midlands asked a local where they could find the famous Spaghetti Junction. 'It's just pasta Birmingham,' he replied.

What do you call an alien in Trafalgar Square?
**Lost.**

Two spacemen landed on Mars and went exploring. 'It's dark, isn't it?' said the first, nervously.

'Certainly is,' agreed the second.

'Er, would you hold my hand, please?' continued the first. 'I can't see where you are.'

'OK,' said the second. 'But take that spiky glove off – it's giving me electric shocks.'

'What spiky glove?' replied the first. 'I'm not wearing any gloves.'

What travels around in a flying saucer but always points north?
**A magnetic alien.**

Knock, knock.
**Who's there?**
Guthrie.
**Guthrie who?**
Guthrie aliens in this flying saucer.

What do you call a nasty alien in a spaceship?
**A waste of space.**

FIRST ALIEN: How long can an alien live without a
brain?
**SECOND ALIEN: I don't know. How
old are you?**

Where would you find an alien's temple?
**On the side of his forehead.**

FIRST SPACEMAN: What kind of
alien is that?
**SECOND SPACEMAN: A
police alien.**
FIRST SPACEMAN: It
doesn't look much like a
police alien to me.
**SECOND SPACEMAN:
Of course not, it's
in plain clothes.**

What's heavier, a full moon or a half moon?
**A half moon, because a full moon is
lighter.**

FIRST ALIEN: My instructor says passing my flying test will be a close thing.
**SECOND ALIEN: Why's that?**
FIRST ALIEN: Because I've got three more lessons and they've only got two more flying saucers.

Knock, knock.
**Who's there?**
Lucinda.
**Lucinda who?**
Lucinda space helmet, I'm suffocating.

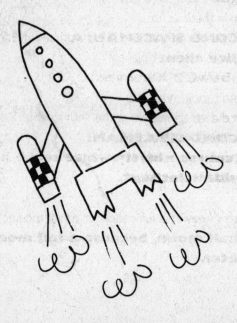

Knock, knock.
**Who's there?**
Norman.
**Norman who?**
Norman has ever set
foot on Jupiter.

What do you call the Jedi teacher
who sits on the floor with his legs
crossed?
**Yoga.**

Did you hear about the alien woman who fell in
love with a cricket player?
**He bowled her over.**

And did you hear about the short-sighted alien who
fell in love with a piano?
**It had such lovely white teeth he
couldn't resist it.**

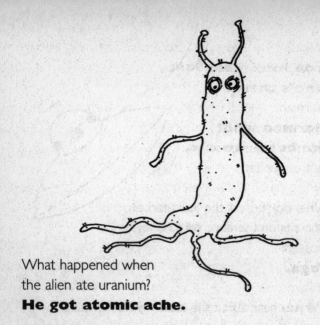

What happened when
the alien ate uranium?
**He got atomic ache.**

FIRST ALIEN: Will you join me in a glass of iced
rocket fuel?
**SECOND ALIEN: Do you think there'll
be room for both of us?**

TOMMY: I just met an alien with no nose.
**TIMMY: How did he smell?**
TOMMY: Terrible!

PROUD ALIEN FATHER: My wife's just had a baby
and it looks just like me.
**HIS FRIEND: Never mind, just as long
as it's healthy.**

What's huge, green and sits around moaning all day?
**The Incredible Sulk.**

What happened when the silly alien listened to the match?
**He burnt his ear.**

What happens if a three-metre-tall, two-metre-wide alien sits in front of you at the cinema?
**You miss most of the film.**

What did E.T.'s mother say to him when he got home?
**'Where on Earth have you been?'**

What's the best way to
speak to an alien?
**From a very long
distance.**

# Monstrous!

What's the difference between
a space monster and a biscuit?
**You can't dip a space
monster in your tea.**

How does a space monster
count up to 17?
**On its fingers.**

What happened when the boy
space monster met the girl space monster?
**It was love at first fright.**

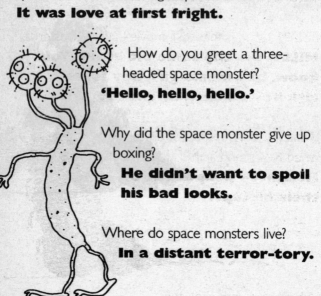

How do you greet a three-
headed space monster?
**'Hello, hello, hello.'**

Why did the space monster give up
boxing?
**He didn't want to spoil
his bad looks.**

Where do space monsters live?
**In a distant terror-tory.**

SALLY: I went with my new boyfriend to see that new space monster film.

**SUSIE: What was he like?**

SALLY: Oh, three metres tall, two green heads, a bolt through his neck . . .

**SUSIE: I meant your new boyfriend.**

SALLY: So did I.

Which science fiction film was about a cricket match with an angry referee?

**The Umpire Strikes Back.**

BILLY: How was that sci-fi movie you saw yesterday?

**MILLY: Oh, the same old story. You know, boy meets girl, boy loses girl, boy builds new girl . . .**

What job did the space monster do when he visited Earth?

**He scared people out of their hiccups.**

What happened when the space monster had a brain transplant?

**The brain rejected him.**

What do you call a space monster with three heads, four feet and 23 noses?
**Very ugly!**

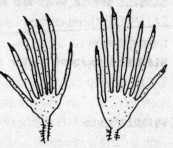

MOTHER SPACE
MONSTER: Don't
eat with your fingers,
Algernon, use a shovel
like I taught you.

FEMALE ALIEN: That space
monster just rolled his eyes at me.
**HER FRIEND: Then roll them back
again.**

What do you call a space monster who sleeps with the windows open?
**A fresh-air fiend.**

Did you hear about the space monster who thought he had bad eyesight?
**He discovered it was all right when he got his hair cut.**

How do you get 22 space monsters in a phone box?
**You open the door.**

Why did Frankenstein's monster get indigestion?
**He bolted his food down.**

OLLIE: Did you hear there's an alien working in the greengrocer's?
**MOLLY: No!**
OLLIE: Yes. He's about three metres tall and two metres wide. Can you guess what he weighs?
**MOLLY: No.**
OLLIE: Fruit and veg.

What did Frankenstein's monster say when he was struck by lightning?
**'Thanks, I needed that.'**

FIRST MONSTER: Why do you say Dr Frankenstein is funny?
**SECOND MONSTER: He keeps me in stitches.**

Why was Dr Frankenstein never lonely?
**He was good at making friends.**

What's the difference between a flea-ridden space monster and a bored guest?
**One's going to itch; the other's itching to go.**

A space monster and a zombie went to an undertaker's. The space monster said, 'I'd like to order a coffin for a friend who's just died.'

The undertaker looked at them. 'Fine,' he said, 'but you didn't need to bring him with you.'

Which space monster makes strange noises in its throat?
**A gargoyle.**

What's the best way of avoiding infection from biting space monsters?
**Don't bite any.**

Two space monsters were talking over their problems. Said the first, 'I'm afraid I'm always pulling ugly faces.'

'That doesn't sound too serious,' replied the second.

'No, but the owners of the faces don't like it when I pull them.'

Why was the space monster called Isaiah?
**Because one of his eyes was 'igher than the other.**

Knock, knock.
**Who's there?**
Ivan.
**Ivan who?**
Ivan to hear you scream.

BABY SPACE MONSTER: I wish we could have a waste disposal unit like other families.

**MOTHER SPACE MONSTER: Shut up and keep eating.**

What looks like a space monster yet isn't a space monster?

**A photograph of a space monster.**

Did you hear about the space monster who won first prize at the Hallowe'en fancy dress dance?

**He cheated, he wasn't wearing a mask.**

What do you call a space monster who's three-metres high, weighs 100 kilos, and has three heads, all with very large teeth?

**Sir!**

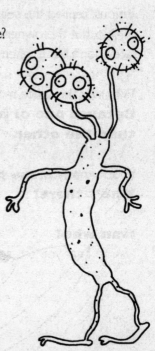

Two space monsters who had landed on Earth looked up at the sky. 'Is that the sun or the moon?' they asked a passer-by.

The man looked up. 'I don't know,' he replied, 'I don't live round here either.'

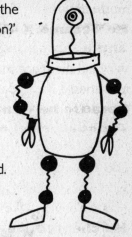

The space monster could be friends with anyone he pleased. The trouble was, he didn't please anyone.

'That space monster hasn't an enemy in the world, but all his friends hate him.'

How do you get a space monster in a matchbox?
**Take the matches out first.**

What happened to Ray when he met a space
monster?

**He became X-Ray.**

Why did the space monster sit on the bag of
tomatoes?

**Because he wanted to play squash.**

# Star-studded

What do you call a robot who always goes the longest way round on a journey?
**R2 Detour.**

What do you call the Star Wars character who spends his time walking into the sea?
**Darth Wader.**

What do you get if you cross a Jedi teacher with a cartoon animal?
**Yoda Bear.**

What do they sing on Mr Spock's birthday?
**'For ears a jolly good fellow.'**

Where was Han Solo when the lights went out?
**In the dark.**

How many letters are there in the aliens' alphabet?
**Twenty-four – E.T. went home.**

Who makes faces at Luke Skywalker and Han Solo?
**Princess Leer.**

What happens if you throw moondust at Jar Jar Binks?

**Jar Jar Blinks.**

A man sat in a pub playing chess with an alien, who had huge green eyes and was dressed from head to foot in a shiny silver costume. A stranger came in and watched them. When the game was over, and the alien had won, the stranger came over and introduced himself.

'Good evening,' he said, 'I'm a film director. That was a very impressive game of chess. Your alien friend could make a fortune in Hollywood, you know.'

'Oh, I don't know,' replied the man, 'today was a fluke. I usually beat him nine times out of ten.'

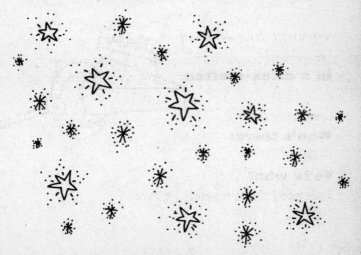

FIRST ALIEN: My girlfriend has beautiful green hair all down her back.

**SECOND ALIEN: Pity it's not on her head.**

Where does Dr Who buy his cheese?
**In a dalek-atessen.**

cheddar

Knock, knock.
**Who's there?**
Felix.
**Felix who?**
Felix cited about meeting Dr Who.

When can an alien travel
as fast as a space rocket?
**When he's inside it.**

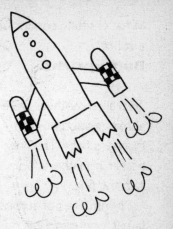

Knock, knock.
**Who's there?**
Dishes.
**Dishes who?**
Dishes the Cybermen,
we've come to get you.

ALIEN WIFE: I think I hear intruders down in the
flying-saucer park. Are you awake?
**ALIEN HUSBAND: No.**

Did the bionic alien have a brother?
**No, just lots of trans-sisters.**

Why did the alien have a whoopee cushion on his
head?
**Because the joke was on him.**

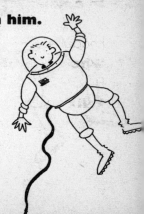

Knock, knock.
**Who's there?**
Who.
**Who who?**
Not Who who, Dr Who!

What is sitting comfortably to a robot?
**Bolt upright.**

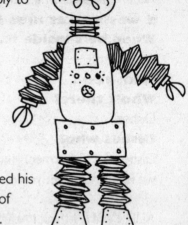

Two alien mothers were admiring another alien mother's baby. 'They say he has his father's looks,' said the first.

'Mmm, I'm not surprised his father wanted to get rid of them,' replied the second.

Two spacemen had embarked from their craft and were exploring the unknown planet when they spotted an angry-looking band of aliens. 'Quick,' said the first, 'send an SOS signal to the spacecraft.' 'An SOS signal,' mused the second spaceman. 'How do you spell that?'

FEMALE ALIEN: Will you still love me when I'm old and ugly?
**MALE ALIEN: I do now, don't I?**

What happened when the vampire met the alien?
**It was love at first bite.**

What smells most on Mars?
**Your nose.**

An alien waved to another alien, whom he'd just spotted. As the second creature came closer, he called out, 'Oh, it's you. I thought you were yourself but now you've come closer I can see that you're your brother.'

What goes 'mooz, mooz'?
**A space rocket flying backwards.**

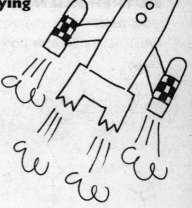

Did you hear about the girl alien who wasn't pretty and wasn't ugly? She was pretty ugly.

Knock, knock.
**Who's there?**
Thezza.
**Thezza who?**
Thezza nalien right behind you!

Knock, knock.
**Who's there?**
Ta.
**Ta who?**
Ta-rdis is the name of Dr Who's time machine.

BABY ALIEN: Mummy, am I a real alien?
**MOTHER ALIEN: Of course. Why do
you ask?**
BABY ALIEN: Because I don't like glowing in the
dark.

# Other Worlds

Knock, knock.
**Who's there?**
Jupiter.
**Jupiter who?**
Jupiter your space boots
on the wrong feet?

Knock, knock.
**Who's there?**
York.
**York who?**
York coming back to Mars with us.

SPACEMAN'S WIFE: So you're not going to Venus
for Christmas this year?
**HER FRIEND: No, that
was last year. This
year we're not
going to Pluto.**

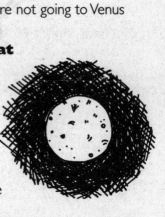

A tourist had been
staying in a hotel on the
moon. As he was leaving, the
hotel manager said to him, 'I
hope you enjoyed your stay, sir.'

'I did,' said the tourist as he was paying the bill.
'But I'm sorry to be leaving the hotel so soon after
practically buying it.'

An alien was booking a hotel room for a holiday on Jupiter. The clerk, taking down details, asked what kind of room he'd like. 'Single, sir?' she said.

'Yes,' replied the alien, 'but I'm getting married next summer.'

ANDY: Did you hear about the alien who heard a good joke when he was on Earth and was going to take it back home with him?

**MANDY: No, what happened?**

ANDY: He decided it would be carrying a joke too far.

Why did the Martian go to the optician?

**He had stars in his eyes.**

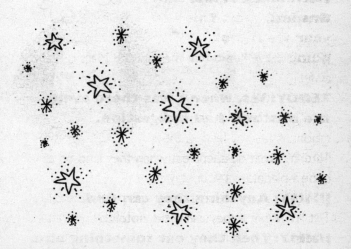

TEACHER: Now, who can point out Mars on this map of the night sky?

**TERRY: There, sir. (Terry points at Mars on the Map.)**

TEACHER: Well done, Terry. Now, Jerry, can you tell me who discovered Mars?

**JERRY: Yes, sir, Terry.**

Are there giant snails on Mars?

**Only if there are giants' toes and fingers there too.**

What's round, purple, and spins through space?

**The Planet of the Grapes.**

FREDDIE: I've heard that the food on Mars is really awful.

**TEDDY: Yes, when I was there even the dustbins had indigestion.**

TIMMY: What do aliens eat when they land on a barren planet?

**JIMMY: Anything they can find.**

TIMMY: What if they can't find anything?

**JIMMY: Then they eat something else.**

Knock, knock.
**Who's there?**
Dismay.
**Dismay who?**
Dismay be an alien, open the door!

Knock, knock.
**Who's there?**
Philip.
**Philip who?**
Philip the rocket, I'm off to the moon.

FIRST ALIEN ON EARTH: I think I need glasses.
**SECOND ALIEN ON EARTH: You certainly do, you're talking to a telegraph pole.**

An alien visiting Earth wanted to go and see the Equator, but he thought he'd better take his laser gun and spacesuit. 'Why do you need them?' asked his friend.

'For protection,' answered the alien.

'From what?' asked his friend.

'Well, the Equator's a lion in the middle of the Earth, isn't it?'

Did you hear about the alien who stayed up all night to work out what happened to the sun when it set? It finally dawned on him.

An alien who landed in the English countryside was surprised to hear two cows talking. 'I hope I don't catch mad cow disease,' said the first.

'Oh, you don't need to worry about that,' replied the second.

'Why not?'

'It doesn't affect us pigs.'

Why will the world never come to an end?
**Because it's round.**

SPACE TRAFFIC CONTROL: Please tell me your height and position.
**SPACE PILOT: I'm 1.5 metres tall and I'm sitting at the control panel.**

An alien walked into a café and ordered a strawberry milk shake. Thinking he wouldn't know anything about money, the proprietor charged him £5 for it. As the alien was paying, the proprietor said, conversationally,

'We don't get many aliens in here.'

'With strawberry milk shakes at £5 a time I'm not surprised,' replied the alien.

What was the alien doing on the motorway?
**About 70 kph.**

An Earthling decided to take his alien friend fishing with him. When he got home he complained to his wife that he hadn't caught anything, and that he'd never take the alien with him again. 'Why?' asked his wife. 'Did he make a noise and frighten away all the fish?'

'No,' replied the Earthling, 'he ate all the bait.'

If a space rocket crashed on the borders of Canada and the USA where would the survivors be buried?
**Nowhere, because the survivors would still be alive.**

Why was the alien called Wonder Boy at school?
**Because everyone else used to look at him and wonder.**

What's woolly, covered in chocolate and travels round the sun?
**A Mars baa.**

GIRL ALIEN: That alien's got pedestrian eyes.
**HER FRIEND: What do you mean?**
GIRL ALIEN: They look both ways before they cross.

Where are all aliens beautiful?
**In the dark.**

Knock, knock.
**Who's there?**
May.
**May who?**
May the force be with you!

Why did the alien take a bath?
**So he could make a clean getaway.**

Did you hear about the alien who sent his photo to a Lonely Hearts Club?
**They sent it back saying they weren't that lonely.**

BEN: What's the difference between an Earthling, an alien and a pot of glue?

**KEN: Well, an Earthling lives on Earth and an alien in outer space, but I don't know about the pot of glue.**

BEN: I thought that's where you'd get stuck.

What did the alien say to the petrol pump?

**'Take your finger out of your ear when you're talking to me.'**

Did you hear about the alien who rode a bike that went round biting people?

**It was known as the vicious cycle.**

Why did the alien wear a bullet-proof vest?

**Because of all the shooting stars.**

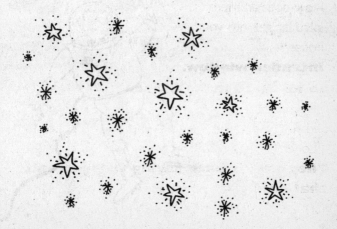

FIRST SPACEMAN: That spacesuit fits you like a bandage.

**SECOND SPACEMAN: Yes, I got it by accident.**

Why did the alien girl walk sideways?

**Her boyfriend had told her she had a beautiful profile.**

How can an alien stop a cold in his head from going to his chest?

**Tie a knot in his neck.**

Why don't astronauts keep their jobs for very long?

**Because as soon as they start they're fired.**

How does an alien intruder get into your house?

**Intruder window.**

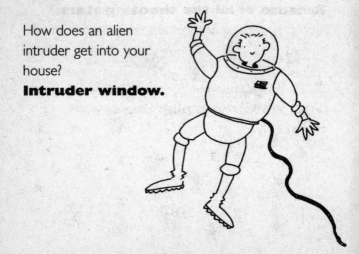

Two aliens were discussing their youth. 'I was very naughty,' said the first.

'So was I,' agreed the second. 'I was the kind of young alien my mother told me not to play with.'

ALIEN'S MUM: Why are you crying?
**LITTLE ALIEN: Because Bill's lost his laser gun.**
MUM: But if he's lost his gun why are you crying?
**LITTLE ALIEN: Because I was playing with it when he lost it.**

'You know, the story that alien dogs can talk is rubbish. If you find an alien dog who says it can talk, it's lying.'

MOLLY: Look, that star up there is Mars.
**DOLLY: Really? Which one is Pa's, then?**

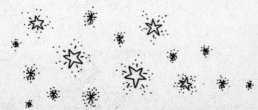

Knock, knock.

**Who's there?**

Thesis.

**Thesis who?**

Thesis an alien with a laser gun, you'd better come out!

# Earthlings
# Strike Back

An alien on Earth fell into a pond. 'Help!' he shouted. 'I can't swim!'

'So what?' said an alien on the shore. 'I can't fly to Mars but I'm not shouting about it!'

A man who thought he was an alien had been to see his doctor. 'I feel much better now,' he said. 'In fact, I'm just like my old self again.'

'In that case,' replied the doctor, 'you must need more treatment.'

Two spacemen were exploring an unknown planet. They'd heard that vicious creatures lived on the planet, but hadn't met any. Nevertheless, they were on their guard. They crept around, peering round vegetation and into craters. It was eerily silent, until, suddenly, they heard a knocking sound. 'Sshh,' said the first spaceman, 'can you hear that knocking? Do you suppose it's one of those vicious space creatures?'

'No,' gulped the second, 'actually, it's my knees.'

Knock, knock.
**Who's there?**
Shirley.
**Shirley who?**
Shirley you know what a
real alien looks like!

An alien went to see a doctor because he kept bumping into things.

'You need spectacles,' was the doctor's verdict.

'Will I be able to read with them?' asked the alien.

'Of course,' replied the doctor.

'Great!' exclaimed the alien. 'I didn't know how to before!'

A spaceman was trying to cheer up a colleague who was feeling a bit fed up. 'Whenever I'm down in the dumps,' he said brightly, 'I get myself a new spacesuit.'

His colleague looked at him. 'Hmm,' he replied, 'I always wondered where you got them from.'

How can you tell if there's an alien in your fridge?
**You can't shut the door.**

An alien on his first visit to Earth stopped a man in the street and asked him the time. 'Two-thirty,' replied the man.

'Don't try being funny with me,' said the alien crossly.

'What do you mean?' asked the man.

'Well,' said the alien, 'I've been asking people the time all day and everyone's given me a different answer.'

A little boy went into a shop. 'How much are those model aliens in the window?' he asked.

'£5 for two, or £3 for one,' answered the shopkeeper.

'I've only got £2,' said the little boy, 'can I have the other one?'

Why did the cyclops alien only pay half his TV licence?
**Because he only had one eye.**

FIRST SPACEMAN: Be careful with that laser! You only just missed shooting me!

**SECOND SPACEMAN: Oh, I'm sorry, I'll aim better next time!**

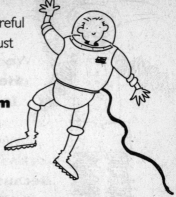

Did you hear about the silly alien who went to a mind-reader and paid to have his thoughts read? **The mind-reader gave him his money back.**

EARTHLING: Was the food I gave you too hot? **ALIEN: No, smoke always comes out of my ears when I eat.**

The young alien army was being drilled. 'Where's your laser gun?' the instructor asked one young recruit.

'I haven't got none,' he replied.

'We don't say that,' retorted the instructor. 'We say, "I do not have a laser gun,"; "You do not have a laser gun,"; "He does not have a laser gun,"; "We do not have a laser gun,"; and so on. Do you understand?'

'No,' replied the recruit. 'And anyway, where have all the laser guns gone to?'

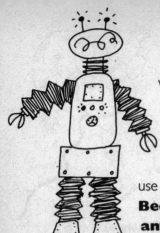

Why was the robot so silly?
**He had a screw loose.**

Why do bald aliens never use keys?
**Because they haven't any locks.**

**JOHNNY: What's the difference between an alien and a post box?**
DONNY: I don't know.
**JOHNNY: Then I'm not sending you out to post my Christmas cards.**

Why did the alien scratch himself?
**Because no one else knew where he itched.**

FIRST ALIEN: When I die I'm leaving my brain to science.
**SECOND ALIEN: Well, I suppose every little helps.**

Alien brain

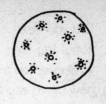

Knock, knock.

**Who's there?**

Juno.

**Juno who?**

Juno where all these aliens came from?

Knock, knock.

**Who's there?**

Soup.

**Soup who?**

Soup-erman.

Knock, knock.

**Who's there?**

Scot.

**Scot who?**

Scot three heads and six arms and I think it must be an alien.

When are you glad to be down and out?

**After a rough flight in a space rocket.**

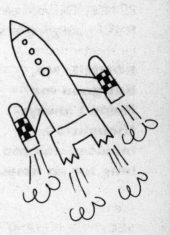

Did you hear about the alien who invented a new pill? It was 50 per cent aspirin and 50 per cent glue – for aliens who had splitting headaches.

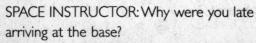

SPACE INSTRUCTOR: Why were you late arriving at the base?

**NEW RECRUIT: I'm not late, I just took my lunch break before coming to work.**

RONNIE: Did you hear that Martians are going on strike for shorter hours?

**BONNIE: No, but good for them. I always thought 60 minutes was too long for an hour.**

Where are aliens found?
**They're so clever they're not often lost.**

FIRST ALIEN: What time did your clock stop?
**SECOND ALIEN: I don't know, I wasn't there.**

TEACHER: Give me a sentence with 'centimetre' in it.
**SHEILA: Susie came back from her holiday on Mars and I was centimetre.**

What does an alien get if he crosses a computer with an elastic band?

**A computer that makes snap decisions.**

BETTY: Why do you call that Martian an executive alien?

**HETTIE: He takes two hours for lunch.**

BRENDA: Was that alien you went out with polite?

**GLENDA: I'll say so. He always took his shoes off before putting his feet on the table.**

BRENDA: And was he a good dancer?

**GLENDA: He'd have been a wonderful dancer if it hadn't been for three things.**

BRENDA: What were they?

**GLENDA: His feet!**

How did the young alien get his hands so dirty?
**He washed his face with them.**

UNCLE ALIEN: And what are you going to do when you're as big as your father?
**BABY ALIEN: Go on a diet.**

FIRST ALIEN: I'm so thirsty my tongue's hanging out.
**SECOND ALIEN: I thought you were wearing a red tie.**

Knock, knock.
**Who's there?**
Fred.
**Fred who?**
Are you Fred of aliens?

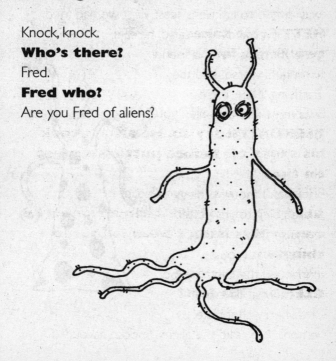

Knock, knock.

**Who's there?**

Heidi.

**Heidi who?**

Heidi clare war on aliens.

How did the alien get a black eye?

**He was hit by a guided muscle.**

An Earthling was telling his friend about the time he
was invited to an aliens' feast. 'First we had fried
robot's liver and slime salad,' he said.

'Ugh!' remarked his friend.

'It gets worse,' said the
Earthling. 'Next there
was roast android and
boiled rats' brains.'

'Ughghghgh!' squealed
the friend.

'Then I thought things
were going to get better,
because they said the
dessert was mousse,'
continued the Earthling. 'So
I asked what flavour –
strawberry, chocolate,
lemon? "No," said the aliens, "moose flavour."'

When is a window like a star?
**When it's a skylight.**

Did you hear about the
three aliens who got jobs
washing up in a restaurant?
One washed, one
dried and the
third picked up
the pieces.

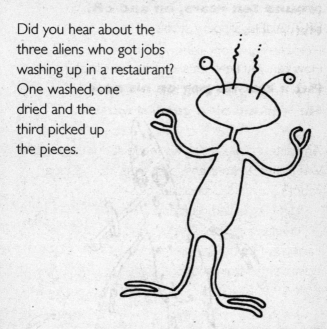

What belongs to an alien but is used more by
others?
**His name.**

Why did the alien take his nose apart?
**To see how it ran.**

FIRST ALIEN: Can you play the piano?
**SECOND ALIEN: Yes, I've played it for around ten years, on and off.**
FIRST ALIEN: Slippery stool?

How can you keep an alien from smelling?
**Put a clothes peg on his nose.**

# Aliens All

How does an alien shave?
**With a laser blade.**

Can an alien jump higher than the Millennium Dome?
**Yes, the Millennium Dome can't jump.**

What do you get if you cross an alien with an owl?
**Something that scares everyone but doesn't give a hoot.**

An elderly alien was putting on weight. 'I'm getting worried about my figure,' she said.

'You'll have to diet,' said her friend.

'Yes,' she sighed, 'but what colour?'

Knock, knock.
**Who's there?**
Ann.
**Ann who?**
Ann Droid.

Knock, knock.
**Who's there?**
Bet.
**Bet who?**
Bet you wouldn't believe an alien is knocking on your door!

Why did the alien wear brown boots?
**Because his black ones were at the mender's.**

What's a robot alien's favourite supper?
**Fish and silicon chips.**

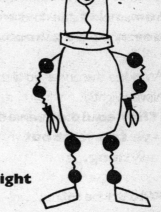

Why was the alien an electrician?
**He liked a bit of light relief.**

Why did the alien cross the road?
**Because he was following the chicken.**

Why are mad aliens like biscuits?
**Because they're crackers.**

Why do aliens wear dark glasses?
**So no one can recognize them.**

What do you get if you cross an alien with a fridge?
**I don't know, but when you take its helmet off you can't see for the light shining in your eyes.**

An alien found a shopping bag full of fish in a London street. He took it to a police station where he was told that if no one claimed it after six months it would be his.

Why did the one-eyed aliens always fight?
**They could never see eye to eye about anything.**

Why did the robot yawn?
**He was suffering from metal fatigue.**

Why did the robot stop smoking?
**He had his fusebox repaired.**

What goes ha, ha, ha, crash?
**An alien laughing his head off.**

FIRST ALIEN: How do you feel today?
**SECOND ALIEN: The same as ever,
with my robot hands.**

MIKE: Did you know that aliens do a dance called the Lift?
**SPIKE: Really? Why's it called that?**
MIKE: It hasn't any steps.

Who won the aliens' beauty
contest?
**Nobody.**

Three hard-of-hearing
aliens met one day. 'Windy,
isn't it?' said the first.
    'No, it's Thursday,' said
the second.
    'So am I,' said the third.
'Let's go and have a cup
of tea.'

What do seafaring aliens eat?
**Fish and ships.**

Why did the one-eyed alien teacher give up his job?
**He didn't see the point in going on
with just one pupil.**

Why did the robot eat little bits of metal all day?
**It was his staple diet.**

Knock, knock.
**Who's there?**
Accordion.
**Accordion who?**
Accordion to the newspapers aliens have landed.

Knock, knock.
**Who's there?**
Ammonia.
**Ammonia who?**
Ammonia little alien and I can't reach the doorbell.

Knock, knock.
**Who's there?**
Orange.
**Orange who?**
Orange you glad I'm not an alien?

What kind of alien has the best hearing?
**The eeriest.**

Where do aliens with bad coughs go in the evenings?
**To the theatre.**

An alien landed in southern England. 'Can you tell me the way to Bath?' he asked a passing policeman.

'I always use soap and hot water,' the officer replied.

ALIEN DAD: I'm worried about my son. He thinks he's a lift.
**ALIEN PSYCHIATRIST: Tell him to come up and see me sometime and I'll have a chat with him.**
ALIEN DAD: I can't, he doesn't stop at this floor.

What's a giant alien's favourite tale?
**A tall story.**

An alien was having singing lessons. 'You should be on the radio,' said her friend.

'Ooh, do you think I'm that good?' she asked, pleased with herself.

'No, I think you're terrible, but if you were on the radio I could switch you off.'

How can you tell if an alien's been in your fridge?
**By the little bits of metal in the butter.**

What kind of coat does a four-handed alien wear?
**A coat of arms.**

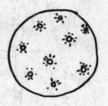

FIRST ALIEN: There were eight stupid aliens called Doh, Re, Fah, Soh, Lah, Ti, Doh.
**SECOND ALIEN: What about Mi?**
FIRST ALIEN: Sorry, I forgot about you.

SIX-HANDED ALIEN: I don't know what to get my husband for his birthday.

**HER FRIEND: Do what I did, get him three pairs of gloves.**

Why did the alien think there was something wrong with his finger?

**Every time he put it in his ear he went deaf.**

ALIEN, TO EARTHLING GARDENER: Do you have a potato patch?

**EARTHLING GARDENER: Why, have you got a torn potato?**

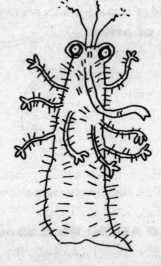

After landing in Britain
five aliens stood
under one very
small umbrella but
none of them got
wet. Why?
**It wasn't raining!**

What happened to
the alien who stole
a calendar?
**He got twelve months.**

A man who kept a clothing
store reported to the police that
an alien had stolen six
pullovers, ten shirts and
a pair of trousers. 'Did
you chase after him?' asked
the policeman.

   'No,' replied the shopkeeper, 'they were my
trousers.'

What kind of alien has the biggest space helmet?
The one with the biggest head!

ALIEN: Do you know why us aliens from Pluto wear yellow boots?

**EARTHLING: No.**

ALIEN: So we can hide upside down in bowls of custard. You've never found an alien in a bowl of custard, have you?

**EARTHLING: No.**

ALIEN: That shows how well it works, then, doesn't it?

## SANDY RANSFORD

# THE
# KNOCK KNOCK
## JOKE BOOK

*Hundreds of hilarious knock knock jokes . . .*

**Knock Knock**
Who's there?
**Mabel.**
Mabel who?
**Mabel doesn't ring, either.**

**Knock Knock**
Who's there?
**Stan.**
Stan who?
**Stan back, I'm coming in.**

**Knock Knock**
Who's there?
**Orson.**
Orson who?
**Orson cart.**

**Knock Knock**
Who's there?
**Sincerely.**
Sincerely who?
**Sincerely this morning I've been waiting
for you to open this door.**

# SANDY RANSFORD

# 2001

## A JOKE ODYSSEY

### The Millennium Joke Book

*2001 side-splittingly funny jokes for the millennium ...*

**Why did the lobster blush?**
Because the seaweed.

**What do cannibals do at a wedding?**
Toast the bride and groom.

**What can a whole apple do that half
an apple can't do?**
Look round.

**Why was the mushroom invited
to lots of parties?**
He was a fungi to be with.

**Why is a football stadium cool?**
Because there's a fan in every seat.

**What do you call a vicar on a motorbike?**
Rev.

What better way to celebrate the millennium than
with this hilarious collection of jokes guaranteed to
make you giggle?

# A selected list of titles available from Macmillan and Pan Books

The prices shown below are correct at the time of going to press. However, Macmillan Publishers reserve the right to show new retail prices on covers which may differ from those previously advertised.

| | | |
|---|---|---|
| **The Knock Knock Joke Book** | 0 330 37514 8 | £2.99 |
| **Spooky Jokes**<br>Sandy Ransford | 0 330 39061 9 | £2.99 |
| **2001: A Joke Odyssey**<br>The Millennium Joke Book<br>Sandy Ransford | 0 330 34988 0 | £3.99 |
| **School Jokes**<br>Sandy Ransford | 0 330 39222 0 | £2.99 |
| **Absolutely Mental 1**<br>Rowland Morgan | 0 330 48172 X | £2.99 |
| **Absolutely Mental 2**<br>Rowland Morgan | 0 330 48173 8 | £2.99 |

All Macmillan titles can be ordered at your local bookshop or are available by post from:

**Book Service by Post**
**PO Box 29, Douglas, Isle of Man IM99 1BQ**

Credit cards accepted. For details:
Telephone: 01624 675137
Fax: 01624 670923
E-mail: bookshop@enterprise.net

**Free postage and packing in the UK.**
Overseas customers: add £1 per book (paperback)
and £3 per book (hardback).